A N STARTING PLACE

*A study of how
men become
mature in
Christ through
relationships*

Jack Hayford

THOMAS NELSON PUBLISHERS
Nashville • Atlanta • London • Vancouver

Published in Nashville, Tennessee, by Thomas Nelson, Inc., Publishers, and distributed in Canada by Word Communications, Ltd., Richmond, British Columbia, and in the United Kingdom by Word (UK), Ltd., Milton Keynes, England.

ISBN 0-7852-7792-7

Printed in the United States of America

1 2 3 4 5 6 7 - 01 00 99 98 97 96 95

*This message was originally brought at
The Church On The Way.*

*It has since been edited and revised
for publication by Pastor Hayford,
in partnership with Pastor Bob Anderson,
Director of Pastoral Relations.*

TABLE OF CONTENTS

DEDICATION

I dedicate this opening book of this series to the thousands of men whom I've already watched set their sights on the high call of God in Christ our Lord--and follow it!

And I express thanks also to Bob Anderson, a man I've seen "truly 'become'" an effective agent of Christ in many circles of influence; and whose gifts and skills brought this book to completion. (He also is the writer of the sections on "All In The Doing" and the Devotional guide on 1 Samuel.)

I desire therefore that the men pray everywhere, lifting up holy hands, without wrath and doubting; in like manner also, that the women adorn themselves in modest apparel, with propriety and moderation, not with braided hair or gold or pearls or costly clothing, but, which is proper for women professing godliness, with good works. Let a woman learn in silence with all submission. And I do not permit a woman to teach or to have authority over a man, but to be in silence. For Adam was formed first, then Eve. And Adam was not deceived, but the woman being deceived, fell into transgression. Nevertheless she will be saved in childbearing if they continue in faith, love, and holiness, with self-control.

— 1 Timothy 2:8-15 (NKJV)

CHAPTER ONE:
GOD'S STARTING PLACE

It was Illinois-in-February, zero-biting *cold* as I walked down the small country path through snow a foot deep.

I was in the Midwest part of our nation to fulfill a speaking engagement, and have to admit the reason I was so enjoying that winter scene was very basic: I had *flown in* to speak, and could *fly right out* when I was done! It's called "Winter on demand"-- without pain!!

It was about 7:30 in the morning, and as I trudged along--earmuffs, scarf, heavy cap, and jacket and all--the sun was rising over the southeast, a purplish orange ball, cresting over snow-laden trees. As bitter as the cold was, it was a delightful, winter-wonderland moment. Even though frozen ice crystals fell as my breath touched the air, the morning was sheer magnificence. It was one of those precious, nonstressed moments, surrounded by God's awesome creation--the kind of moment I'd want to remember on a July day when I'm back driving L.A.'s freeways during rush hour.

As I continued walking--every step a crunch under my feet--I had no idea it was in this scene that God would meet me. I was entirely unprepared for what would become one of the most important assignments ever impressed upon my heart concerning how I was to lead as a pastor, and how I, myself, was to live in the ensuing years. This "prompting" I received from the Lord needs a context to clarify the significance of what He was about to say, so please allow a moment of background information.

Just a year before our small congregation had experienced a dramatic visitation of God's grace. In just one year from that point of visitation we'd quadrupled--grown from 100 people to just over 400. Of course, I hadn't the slightest dream that our church would take on the "mega" proportions it eventually has--serving 8,000 to 10,000 people in public services each week. The 400 was "plenty of miracle" for me!

But that morning, as my feet crunched the frozen country pathway, my heart was full. I'd seen a year of incredible blessing, and with that, here I was amid the beauty that surrounded me at that moment.

It was then that the words came:

"I want you to begin to gather men and to train them. As you do, I will raise up strong leadership for the future of this church."

Though I didn't understand all the implications at that moment, I did sense God's desire to build men--strong men, strong single guys, strong husbands, strong fathers who knew who they were. *"Gather the men and begin to teach them."*

Our "Men's Growth" Starting Place

It was about six weeks later I began the monthly men's meetings: Men's Growth Seminars. The first time we ever planned to meet, I made a direct invitation to thirty-five men; sending each a note, as well as putting a general announcement in the church bulletin. Of those I invited, eighteen came. So, we made a circle of chairs--a simple, up-close-and-together arrangement. We had a time of worship, and then I opened my heart to them about God's "word" to me. And that's how it started.

So, what happened that Illinois wintertime morning affected not only my life, but drastically--and very beautifully--the whole of the congregation I serve. For that event to which I'm referring, over 20 years ago, made an impact so great it still resonates through and orchestrates my thoughts, pastoral values, and ministry.

Over the years there have been multiplied thousands who have been influenced-- thousands of men who have been transformed. The direct result is that as our church has grown, there have been stable underpinnings, not only through vital Christ-exalting worship and Word-centered preaching, but by the roles filled with a cadre of committed, growing, sensible, submitted, godly men. Why should or why could such a strategy make so much difference?

The Issue of Creational and Redemptive "Sequence"

Let me make a head-on statement at the risk of generating sparks. In our sometimes militantly feminist society, it's more than likely that some people won't listen no matter how carefully I explain. But to begin, let me say: In most of His workings, God *starts* with men. Get that. *Men* are God's "starting place."

Fundamental to our whole study is this fact: *The shaping of a man is foundational to anything God seeks to do.*

I am in no way suggesting that men are superior to women. Neither am I hinting at any rejection or reduction of the value of women in God's Kingdom purposes. But this starts with a simple fact in Scripture--the *sequence in creation:* "*Adam was formed first*" (1 Tim. 2:13); and it's this sequence which God has chosen to preserve in His redemptive "order" of dealing with humankind.

There's a functional purpose to that order. It isn't that by making man first He prefers him. It *is* that *having* made man first

12

in the *initial* creation, He has chosen to deal with man first in His quest to recover what the Fall has brought about. Just as God in Creation's purpose started with man (in order to later form woman from his side, and thereby demonstrate the union and heart-commitment He intended the couple to have), so in redemption's purposes He begins with men to demonstrate something. That *"something"* is the objective of our whole study--the target of our men's ministries. Our objective is to recover something of understanding we men have lost about our responsibilities under God. But more about that later.

Right now, however, let it be made very clear--indeed it's obvious!--that God has not perpetuated this order or sequence because men are wiser, or more intelligent, or more gifted--or *anything else*--more than women.

For example, if we were to take a cross-sampling of the IQs of a mixed group of men and women, 50% of the women would be more intelligent than the men, more gifted, etc.--and vice versa. And I also want to assert that *some* feminist concerns are valid. It is unfortunate that it's taken our formerly male-dominated society so long to acknowledge the equality of women in many areas. In our Western culture--but even viciously worse in some others--there are still many places where women suffer from dehumanizing sexism and grievous injustice. *That is not part of God's design* and it *is* offensive to His will. Such instances have nothing whatsoever to do with the principle of creational and redemptive *sequence* with which we're dealing.

So, God's dealing with men as His "starting place" has nothing to do with any system that demeans or restricts women. Nonetheless, God has appointed an "order" for processing His work in advancing His redeeming, recovering, releasing works among humanity. And things happen better and they happen faster when they are on God's terms. God starts with men, *not* because men learn better or faster--indeed, we in fact tend *not* to! But this still is God's order, and He has chosen to "initiate" what I'll call "releasing life" through men; i.e., things being released to divine order because men accept their responsibilities under that order. So, we deduce: *There are no second class citizens in God's Kingdom*, but there is a creational order which God has maintained in His redemptive purposes; an order that works best when men learn to accept their responsibility as the Creator intended.

But reactions do arise. Human arrogance still dares to say, "No, God! Don't do it that way. We have new insight. Look at it THIS way!"

The reactionary stance to God's sequential order may rise with accusations of male chauvinism. Others point to the obvious fact that men fail: "So why are they any better

14

than women for God's initiating His work?" And my answer is to emphasize: "Better isn't the issue; God's order or sequence *is.*" We refuse accusations of male chauvinism, stoutly opposing such practices. There is a radical difference between what I'm proposing and what male chauvinism does.

Male chauvinism is essentially the result of granting the *privileges of preference* to men without requiring of them the *responsibilities of leadership.* It's male chauvinism that toys with women and trumpets the hollow idea of men being "better." In contrast to this, we are NOT *persisting* in an argument for male preference or dominance, but *insisting* on a male's acceptance of his responsibilities in leadership. When *that* is realized, the man's "leader" role will never be used to limit or control the advancement or fulfillment of women, but to serve and assist the woman's highest possibilities--including *her* discoveries of leadership, influence, and biblical self-realization.

God's plan is for a man to take his leadership role--to learn of, to accept, and to exercise those *responsibilities* (not privileges) that thereby he might serve and assist God's means for the release of a woman's highest potential.

No! Chauvinists we're not!

In this vein, I believe stark honesty requires a dual admission. First, that Chris-

tianity has done more to recover and equal-
ize the societal gap between men and women,
and thereby to dignify womanhood, than
any other social force or religious system on
earth. Second, however, the same honesty
requires an admission with regret. Some
Christian traditions have in places and at
times, whether intentionally or unwittingly,
fostered some degree of male chauvinism
they have based on a supposed "biblical"
foundation. In seeking to distance ourselves
from that injustice, we nonetheless still hold
to true biblically based teaching. The Spirit
of Truth in the eternal Scriptures shows
God's intent. He points the way toward
prioritizing the development of men--re-
sponsible men--without diminishing anything of a woman's potential. And when this
way is honored, the end result will be the
maximizing of each woman's greatest possibilities at every dimension, just as surely as
it will the man's.

The history-changing invasion of Jesus
Christ into the human scene was to make us
all one and to bring salvation's victories to
every individual, we all--regardless of
gender--are made *winners*, now and forever!
This is the spirit of our whole proposition in
focusing Men's Ministries:

*"There is neither Jew nor Greek, there is
neither slave nor free, there is neither male
nor female; for you are all one in Christ
Jesus"* (Galatians 3:28).

16

Christ has come not only to save us and to break hell's powers, but also to undo social injustice at every level. It's important to recognize that fact, because the above evidence (Gal. 3:28) of God's acknowledgment of equality between men and women tells us something. He not only is set on liberating people so that both men and women can become all that they were intended to be. He has also laid the foundation in His Word as to how this may come about on *His* terms; a plan which starts with His bringing men to learn their role.

Beginning With "A Man"

God is unapologetic about this plan He has of "starting things" with men. It's threaded throughout His Word.

- The human race began with a *man*--Adam.

- The vision of faith's promise--how to walk a pathway of faith with God--began with a *man*--Abraham.

- The Jewish peoples began with a *man*--Jacob; to whom God reached out and called saying: "I will make of you a great nation," and his twelve sons became the fathers of the twelve tribes of Israel.

- Israel's Deliverance from Egypt--which is a grand picture of God's whole deliverance program for all mankind through the blood of the Lamb--came under the leadership of

17

a *man*--Moses.

• Israel's possession of Canaan came under the leadership of the *man*--Joshua; who led the people of God into their inheritance, and became the biblical "type" of Jesus, who as our Leader brings us into the possession of our God-promised destinies.

• The precursor of "Messiah," the royal prototype of the one who would become humanity's King, was a *man*--David; from whose line would come the Savior of mankind, Jesus, later called "the Son of David."

• And finally when God became flesh to rescue all mankind, He came as a *man*--in the form of His Son Jesus Christ; the ultimate *Man*, the Second Adam from Heaven, the Son of God!

In underscoring these facts, I would not, nor could I, dismiss the worth or the preciousness of womanhood. Nothing about God's order reduces the marvelous role of the woman nor suggests a heavenly rejection of her significance. And further and finally, let it be noted that the Bible specifically says, "God is not a man" (Num. 23:19). But neither is He a woman. God is neither male nor female. But *historically* and *redemptively*, God has most commonly led the way--releasing His purposes in the interest of ALL humanity--through the leadership of men.

"Maximum things" don't happen without seeing this "starting place."

TALK ABOUT IT! Chapter questions to explore with a friend.

1) What are four dramatic examples of God choosing men at pivotal moments in human history?

2) Think over how the world has viewed Christianity as chauvinistic. What are some factors you think might have given fuel to this misunderstanding? What key truths have been overlooked by the world mentality in their maintaining such a view?

3) What's a good argument for Christianity being the most dynamic liberating force for women ever? What contrast do you see in other cultures?

4) Do you see the difference between the issue of *sequence* and *preference*; that God's redemptive order is not based on "liking men more," but on "having made man first"?

CHAPTER TWO:
RELATING TO IT ALL!

Take a look. If a church is deficient in spiritual vitality, ask: "What place is being given to the development of men?" I think we'll find it generally true that when God breaks through in a church, it's because He's making a breakthrough with men. Women seem more ready in spiritual responsiveness, and that's a beautiful fact. And the good that happens when they do is no less wonderful for that. But there's a need to come full circle in a holy breakthrough in men. And I believe that's the reason the Lord dealt with me that day. When men are strong in the ways of the Lord, the expansion of the Kingdom of God not only advances, it accelerates. Spiritual manhood affects everything!

• Manhood on God's terms begets a new *single man's mind-set*, which creates a new cultural context with non-self-centered men who don't exploit women, and who understand their own life purpose and thereby serve God effectively.

• Manhood per God's design is foundational to fullest *husbandhood*. It's the beginning of a marriage that works because the man loves his wife as Christ loved the Church and gave Himself up for it.

• Real manhood is also foundational to fullest *fatherhood*. It is the prerequisite for well-adjusted children that they have a happy, "loved" mom, as well as a dad who is diligent to fill his role in the family unit.

• True manhood in Christ also touches the *business world* with unique impact. Men will become successful, knowing who they are as men, and not by reason of a falsely competitive machismo or by manipulative scheming, but instead through God's grace working His highest creative purposes *for* each one, they succeed. And,

• True manhood releases life in *the Church*, as the credibility of the relevance of Christ is manifest; as the notions of "spirituality equals unmanly" or "Christians are wimps" are buried--permanently!

So it is, if *manhood* is diminished, perverted, imbalanced, misunderstood, impotent or destructive--*anything* less than accurately reflective of the image of Christ--then the world takes a loss at every level.

Men in general will tend to be without direction and confidence.

Marriages will tend to become weak or be

dissolved.

Children tend to reproduce the rejection, loneliness or pain they grow up with.

Families tend to be unstable and deficient.

Businesses lose out.

The Church is stultified.

In short, men lead the way, whether for good or no good.

In contrast, understanding God's sequential order concerning men in leadership roles will bring God's release to everyone--men *and* women. True biblical teaching will elevate womanhood. *It will bring a holy freedom to both, men and women, and it will bring an ultimate equality between a husband and wife.*

Defining the Man as Head

The idea of being "head" has been sorely distorted and often exploited. To avert misunderstanding, let's take a quick look at a biblical definition of "the head"; a term which essentially points to the responsible role of the *married* man. But certain of these principles are spiritually true (if not always societally so) irrespective of a man's domestic status.

• "Head" means to provide leadership, not to suppress it; as with benevolent, serv-

22

ing leaders in a society.

- True "headship" serves the interests of those being led; as the physical body's head sees, speaks, hears, and thinks in the interest of the whole body (but without the body even the head is helpless).

- True "headship" is like a soldier "on the point"; as in the way he risks his own safety in the interest of the rest of his squad or platoon.

God never intended the man, as the "head," to be a domineering, dogmatic kind of overlord at work, to his wife, over his kids, or anywhere else. He intended the man to accept the responsibility of leadership. But, fellows, learning *how* that can happen is a difficult thing for every one of us. It's tough stuff for us to find out how we are to relate to each level of God's assigned responsibility and thus become what He intended us to be.

Often, the idea of a man filling his "leading" role is twisted or misconstructed to mean or be applied as some kind of "bossism," or "chief of the fiefdom." This mindset was caricatured in the '50s TV series, "The Honeymooners," a classic which continues with wide acceptance in reruns, both for reasons of comedy as well as its reflection of our human foibles. Jackie Gleason's portrayal of Ralph Kramden was brilliantly hilarious, but also pathetically tinged with that distorted view still existent in some men: "I'm the king of the castle, Alice, and you?--You're nobody!" Remember how he would go on his strutting parade around the kitchen?

Everybody knew that *he* was the real nobody and Alice was who really "ran the store." It's the inevitable reversal resultant from a twisted view of authority. That scenario reflects the truly sad case of the man who doesn't see the failure and foolishness of the "king of the castle" mind-set; who doesn't understand that "to lead" means "to serve." Are there any of us who need to become clearer on this: that our "leading" role is *not* one of superiority, but to become a role of *service? As Jesus Christ our Lord, the Lord of Glory, became a Servant, we are called to be men--as He was*. Let's let Him bring us to the fullness of the discovered power that comes through discovered servanthood.

I sense that right now the whole Church is on the brink of something remarkable. Something new is stirring everywhere, and I sense it uniquely in things I perceive Him seeking to do among men. Jesus is determined to expand the borders of His Kingdom, Sir. And He's calling you and me--*today*--just as He did His disciples long ago! The hell-burnt ruins of Adam I--the fallen man--smolder around us. But Adam II has come to restore all things to the original created order. Let's all--each one of us--be among those men who hear what the Holy Spirit is saying to the Church, and who respond in step with His present redemptive works!

Maintenance, Servicing, and "A Clean Filter"

As men turning to God's redemptive plan, we need to let His wisdom *service us* so that *we* will be prepared to serve. God's "word" to men--to you, Sir, and to me--is "responsibility." He is calling us to accept responsibilities as He teaches us and calls us to responsibly live out what we're made to be. But we'll need His help, just as any equipment needs the helpful benefit of "servicing."

God put us together and He knows how we work. As the Designer and Engineer of our souls, He has prescribed a very specific program of maintenance. That maintenance program is clearly outlined in the Bible--the "Owner's Manual" for human life.

Have you seen the TV commercial of the auto mechanic talking about the need to regularly change your car's oil filter? He summarizes by saying if you don't regularly change the filter every so-many-1000-miles, a combination of things will happen--bad things. He notes that inevitably there will be deficiency in the operation of the engine and that eventually the likelihood of a breakdown is almost certain. So in persuading us to buy the oil filter "up front"--to get your engine serviced and preserve it from breakdown--he says, *"You can pay me now or you can pay me later!"*

I think God wants to get our attention the same way, wanting to service our systems of thought and life. He wants us to experience His "filtering" of our minds so the ways of thinking that characterize our world are filtered out. We men have a propensity to chest thump (at least privately); to suppose our own "do-it-my-way" philosophy is the best, even at the expense of God's ways. But until that "world-think" gets filtered out--until we let God regularly "service" how we think--we're going to pay an incredible debt as the "engine" sputters, or things "break down" in life. But how much better to "get serviced" *now* and get on with God's program. It isn't that God is threatening us with breakdown if we don't do it His way. But we *do* reap what we sow. It's far better to "pay up now" by having our understanding re-tooled and our minds purged of things that confuse and hinder the effective operation of God's system in our lives.

The choice to let God begin His work in you *now* will affect how you think about yourself; will affect how you relate to your friends and family; will affect everything to do with your business; and affect how you relate to matters in the Church--the Body of Christ. We can't afford *not* to be "serviced." No one in his right mind wants to "pay later."

So exactly how does a man choose to let God begin His work in him now?

Three Circles: Relating to It All!

Let's begin with the issue of a man's relationships: how he relates to life, to love, to leading--to it all! The starting place is with pivotal relationships and with relational understanding. Just as *God's* starting point is with men, a *man's* starting place is to find alignment with God's ways in his relationships. There are three primary areas of relationship which are critical in shaping us as men.

• Each of them has unique obstacles that can thwart us.

• Each of them has awesome potential to fulfill us.

• Each of them is so precious that both hell and heaven are intensely interested in possessing them.

These three circles of relationship are paramount to a man's development. The *first* is with God. The *second* is with his wife (or how an unmarried man thinks about eventually marriage). The *third* is with other men.

TALK ABOUT IT! Chapter questions to explore with a friend.

1) What are four areas of life in which men have been specifically ordained for leadership? Into which of these areas would you like to see the Lord move you?

2) Discuss the relationship between "authority," "responsibility," and "servanthood." Give one example of each attribute from Jesus' life.

3) Can you think of viewpoints or practices God may want to begin "filtering" from your thoughts or practice?

CHAPTER THREE:

POURING GOD
A CUP OF COFFEE?

Read with me from Paul's first letter to Timothy, as the Apostle expresses his prayer for Christian men in a graphic picture:

"I desire therefore that men pray every-where lifting up holy hands without wrath and doubting" (1 Timothy 2:8).

That's a noble and manly picture! It clashes with the negative projections of spiritually committed men that the media has etched on our minds. An irresponsible use of stereotypes is so common in the secular media; so often portraying the spiritually inclined male as a pompously pious or heavy-handed religious bigot. With incredible regularity, (barring such rare wonders as *Chariots of Fire*, for example), a man of purposeful religious character is typically shown as devoid of genuineness, who generally turns out to be some "freako" living out the ultimate hypocrisy. A preacher is so often caricatured as frantic--foamingly threatening God's wrath in public, while everything he does in private is either hateful or corrupt, from beating his wife, to blistering his kids, to womanizing parishioners. How often it happens on the screen! The film or video plot ends with the "religious" man as the serial killer or the fake! The message which distills is always the same: (1) "Godly men" are phonies; and (2) God Himself is rendered as irrelevant for *real* men.

But the Bible has another kind of man in mind. The text calls for men with an open commitment to the living reality of His Person and Presence. The phrase, "lift up holy hands without wrath and doubting" calls to a *declarative* stance; it seeks a man who has *discovered a confidence* in his relationship with the Lord. This isn't some dandy dude who struts up to the throne of God, hands swinging upward with a casual or cutesy excitability. No! He's coming with *holy hands*--hands that have had something happen to them. They've been transformed! He comes before the Lord, with a countenance of openness and recognition, knowing that "I am received and accepted by my Father--the Mighty God!"

Paul is saying, "I would that men were like this": men of *faith* (that is, "without doubting") and men of *self-control* (not possessed by anger, "without wrath"). So much unbelief and anger dominates the modern male; unbelief because of ignorance of God's Word, and anger due to uncertainty. Much anger burns because of a low-grade irritation present from a nagging, yet often unidentified, sense of inadequacy--not having realized "something" in life. It's the cry of a man's inner being to seize his destiny, a destiny unfulfilled and seemingly light-years out of reach.

But here is a biblical call to a real relationship--to a friendship with God; to be able to freely come to Him for everything. It's a call to a friendship so intimate, it's as if God drank coffee, you'd pour Him a cup, and feel comfortable coming to Him...and then, to come and pour out your heart as well. Imagine it, just the two of you--God and son, "over coffee"--sitting there, as *friends*. Such a man will learn that his walk with God allows for such "pouring out," for *emptying* anger, pride, lust or anything else eating at him. God doesn't see this as though you're "flinging things" in His face; as though you were putting Him at fault, or as if your failures disallowed forthrightness with Him. Rather, this "pouring out" is a learning to "cast all our care on Him for He cares for us" (1 Peter 5:7).

Please make this distinction: there's a big difference between being "*saved*," as glorious as that is, and *learning* a *walk* with God in friendship. God becomes included in everything in your life. David, that fabulous earthen-vessel who showed us what a heart for God was all about even in the midst of his human frailty, often exhibited in psalm after psalm a great pattern for us to use in prayer.

• Phase I: He cried out, pouring forth his frustrations, fears, and anger at God's feet. But he didn't stop there.

• Phase II: He reaffirmed Who God is and all that God has done for him in the past.

• Phase III: Caught up with the glory of God's faithfulness and majesty, he praised and worshiped. The trash is taken out, the temple is cleansed, and worship is reinstated (check this pattern out in places like Psalms 57, 60, and 77).

This free-to-face-Him call is at the center of Christ's heart for men. Note how Jesus, having walked with His disciples for three years, one day said to them, "No longer do I call you servants...but I call you friends" (John 15:15). The Lord Jesus Himself wants you and me to walk in that intimate a relationship with Him! Praise God!

However, everything about our lives as men seems to work against it!

Not Without a Fight

Let's look at three things that seem to work against a man's possibilities of really having a confident relationship with God.

1. *The Painful Absence of Models.*

I wonder how many who read these words have had a complete absence of anybody to follow; never having someone you could watch in the formative years of your upbringing, about whom you could have said, "That's how a man is supposed to live!" Did you have anyone to watch who showed you a model of a man with peaceful, unfeigned confidence in his relationship with God, of whom you could say, "I want to be just like him!"?

I have heard so many sordid stories of authority figures--potential role models--who failed; fathers or teachers who violated or brutalized people, relatives who mocked or neglected family members, or pastors who seemed like such good guys but then turned out to be dishonest or immoral. Young minds get burned by corrupt images and their hope of just plain "good manhood" withers and dies.

Or maybe you had a good role model, but didn't have the opportunity to get close enough. Relationship with that man who seemed to be what you thought manhood was supposed to be about, never seemed to come within reach or schedule. There was only a kind of quiet distance between you and him, real but remote, like seeing but not being able to span the breadth of the Grand Canyon--nice view, but no touch, no warmth. Or maybe you grew up with a woman as the only leadership model in your life. There's no fault there; certainly no minimizing the worth of a woman's influence. But still you didn't have a *man* to show you the way to *man*hood.

Thus, in the absence of dynamic models to help form our lives according to the Lord's design, many men don't know how to respond as a godly man to life's situations, nor how, for that matter, to be a good role model themselves. Their fractured image of manhood tends to go on reproducing its painful deficiency--one generation after another. *Unless*...unless we break the chain and become God's man. Then, not only do *we* win, but we pass that wholeness on to others--whether to our sons or to other men.

Imagine a boy and his dad on the baseball field. Dad says:

"Now, son, when you go to the plate, you just put your feet about that distance apart...right. Now just take the bat...No, no, Son; just scoot the bat down a little bit. Give about two or three inches there--it's called 'choking the bat.' You'll be able to control your swing better--that's good. Now just take a couple of swings...that's it! Great!"

Think of that kid's advantage. There's somebody there to coach. And when he goes to the plate, whether he gets a hit or not, he'll feel a different degree of assurance--a confidence because *somebody* was there to "coach." And when the same boy goes home and drifts off to sleep at night, there's a faint glow inside. Because that somebody added to his self-worth. A confidence has been ignited that will spill over from baseball into life. Men in formative years need good models.

But there's a second thing that works against our having a confident friendship with God.

2. *The Abounding Presence of Corruption.*

Most men reading these words right now will go to a place of business tomorrow. There, whether it's sophisticated or crude in its tone or delivery, they'll be surrounded by the lewd, the corrupt and the foul. It may be in a pornographic desk calendar, obscene posters, crude speech, sexual innuendos, or coarse jokes. The air is blue with profanity or suggestiveness, and impurity is ever present.

Anyone who's worked as a janitor can tell you there's a world of difference between the women's and the men's restroom walls. The men's are scrawled with foul drawings, filthy words, and phone numbers to call for "action"--either sex available.

Or the corrupt may be business-oriented; the boss wanting you to sell a half-truth to a customer, or "fudge" on accuracy in reported figures.

So much about a man's life is surrounded by corruption, and it works against him. Even if in his heart he says, "I want to be a man that walks with God," he feels like Isaiah: "I am a man of unclean lips, and I live in the middle of a group of people of unclean lips" (Isa. 6:5). The sense of unclean surroundings almost oozes into one's soul--osmosis from a corrupt environment. It brings a terrible disqualifying sense to the serious possibility of a man conceiving of himself as a friend of God.

With the absence of models and the presence of the corrupt, there's a third force that erodes masculine confidence in relating to God.

3. *The Consciousness of Our Own Failure.*

There are none of us who haven't sinned. The Bible says "All have sinned and fallen short of the glory of God" (Rom. 3:23). If we're honest, our souls *more* than agree. Our sins may have been very private and shielded or very public and known. We may even be widely respected and known for our social, occupational or even Christian success or service, yet a dark corner of our soul is still hooked by hell to a particular area of fiendish bondage.

Who among us, right now, may wish that this "hook from hell" could be yanked out; that the "puppet strings" compelling our sinning be cut? How many wish they could erase from mind the inescapable "replays" of pornographic videotapes you saw? Maybe it was only once; that day in a hotel room, far away from home and your family; when buttons were pushed for "late night adult entertainment" (what an insulting use of the word "adult"!) when your mind was invaded, and now your soul seems permanently stained.

You may well already have come to the Lord, have repented, and known He has forgiven you. But *still*, your mind has those scenes riveted in place. And the sad consequence is the awful absence of conviction you feel in your confidence toward God. In such a case, one's perception of his manliness can seem painfully shallow and the term "manhood" can sting with mockery in the presence of such a scarred self-image.

But the Bible doesn't say that friendship with God begins with an accomplished moral perfection. God doesn't mandate a track-record proof showing years of commitment to Him.

Friendship with God starts with coming to Him for forgiveness. In Christ, He banishes our record of failure and declares us "clean!" That's why we can walk into His presence with holy hands uplifted in praise-filled thanks.

"But," somebody says, "you don't know what my hands have done, or what they have touched, and what has rendered them unholy." And I agree, I *don't* know.

But God does.

And He who calls us to friendship with Himself knows something else, and He wants to remind you and me of it:

Whatever our hands have done in sinning, Jesus' hands have cleansed in salvation. And His hands were nailed through in order that your hands and mine might be cleansed by His blood!

Praise His Name--His *scarred* hands will *unscar* ours!!

In fact, let me urge you to take action right now. Would you just put your hands in front of you--there where you are--and say: "Lord Jesus, because of *Your* hands, mine can be holy right now. And I rebuke every spirit of condemnation that would seek to rack my mind or body with guilt!" Then, if you will--as Paul said in our text--lift your hands and praise the Lord "without wrath or doubting"; let *anger* over past failure be done with, and let *doubt* over your acceptance with God be resolved. *Lift up your opened, cleansed hands with praise!* Do it in the confidence that you have full forgiveness of sin, and in the assurance that you can walk in friendship with God in a holiness He'll grow into your character. Friendship with God is a viable possibility with real confidence for one grand, overtowering reason: *the blood of Jesus cleanses from all sin!* (1 John 1:9). That's the basis for our confidence.

TALK ABOUT IT! Chapter questions to discuss with a friend.

1) King David had a pattern of prayer found in a number of psalms. What three phrases characterized that pattern?

2) Name three forces of conflict that work against our having a confident relationship with God.

3) For which area of struggle do you need a brother to pray for you this week? Call and ask him to.

CHAPTER FOUR:

THE DYNAMIC DUO--
YOU AND YOUR WIFE!

Nothing's more pricelessly worth discovering on this earth! And few things are more derided, joked about or doubted-as-beautiful than a man's relationship with his wife.

Even if you're not married, you're going to like this chapter!

It's *so* important to us all--to our understanding our manhood--that I want to have you dig into the subject with a commitment to *think*...to think *deeply*.

In fact, brother, I'm inviting you to school for a chapter or two; because what follows is going to get "teachy." I say that, because I want to plow into a passage of scripture which holds the key to a foundational understanding of this very precious and vital relationship: a man with his wife. I'm asking you to gird up your mind to *think*--to look clearly into God's Word at life-impacting truth. So hang on, and let's go.

Let's start by tackling one of the most

misunderstood passages in the New Testament; verses 9-15 of our text in 1 Timothy, chapter 2. Please open your Bible and note especially the phrases in verses 11 and 12: *"Women adorn themselves in modest apparel...learn in silence with all submission...the woman being deceived..."* Then, also *"I do not permit a woman to teach or to have authority over a man, but to be in silence."*

These have historically been very problematic words, and this passage seems to have muddied relationships between men and women rather than clarified them.

Our objective in seeking to "solve" the tough questions this passage raises is found in the promise which occurs in verse 15:

"Nevertheless she will be saved in childbearing IF THEY continue in faith, love, and holiness, with self-control" (emphasis mine).

You see, in this verse there is a very desirable goal being realized: (1) a marital unity, (2) led by a man, which (3) brings special benefits to his wife and himself. The issue in this verse isn't just "having babies," but finding a fruitfulness in relationship which brings spiritual unity and its practical benefits. So it's worth "figuring out"--worth *studying through* this difficult portion of God's Word to find the fruitful potential of the promised dimensions of relationship shown. The goal is a distinct and blessed *partnership* and *friendship* with distinct benefits.

Looking at this text, I ask *every* man, irrespective of marital status, to consider the implications of the Scripture. As difficult as the passage appears initially, it delivers a wealth of ministry and enlightenment once we get over barriers of misunderstanding and distortion. (And I believe that any woman who would hear or read these words--*any* objective thinking person-- would say, "You know, that *does* make sense now that I see that. I didn't realize *that's* what the Bible meant here.")

Two Issues To Address

There are actually two issues in these verses. The second is more direct to our subject--i.e., a man's relationship with his wife. But the first, "modest apparel," rec- ommends explanation lest anyone think either; (a) that this text is not relevant today, or (b) that the Bible is tinged with a sexist condescension toward women. We need to be convinced of the Bible's sensibility and integrity on this issue of a woman's appear- ance, because then we will more easily be- come settled in seeing and honoring God's sane, loving intent for *both* womanhood and manhood. Our grasp of the first issue ("mod- est apparel") will bring the second issue into easier perspective (how a man relates to his wife). And we'll see how "they continue" together in beautiful partnership and with practical blessings.

1. *Propriety, Not Prudery.*

The issue of appropriate apparel is found in verses 9 and 10, wherein Paul challenges "...that women adorn themselves in modest apparel with propriety." He says they should do so "in moderation, not with braided hair or gold or pearls or costly clothing."

Well, do we have a problem!

Somebody's shouting, "Hey, my wife, relative or daughter wears braids! What about it? Cut 'em off?" Somewhere someone's reading this and his wife is a lovely lady sporting a magnificent "corn row"--one of those stylized hairdos with multiple tiny braids all over her head! So, before we go any further--"Everyone, 'Attention!' I want you to know right now that God is *not* arbitrarily 'coming down on the case' of women with braids!"

The "braiding of hair" and the related injunctions in this Bible text were specific confrontations of a cultural context where these feminine styles were employed as a carnal "invitation"--a sort of sexual enticement. The text is not a divine order for a woman to dress like a pilgrim in order to be godly. But it does point to the need for discernment within one's culture; to recognize the difference between carnal dress and otherwise. The text in its time was opposing "dressing to kill"; seeking to be publicly seductive, or to call attention to one's self in a sensual way. In contrast, the Bible says, a Christian woman will know the difference between what is a modest and appropriate dress that's truly beautiful, and what instead is dressing to arouse a man at a sensual level. Looked at within that light, the spirit of the verse is timeless.

2. When "Silence" May Be Golden.

Now we're ready for the "husband-wife relationship" part of this text. But strangely, it begins with a really tough nut to crack. Look at verses 11 and 12:

"Let a woman learn in silence with all submission. And I do not permit a woman to teach or to have authority over a man but to be in silence."

How could this demand build relationship!? Verses like this have been wielded with feminist fury and legalistic glee. It's the kind of stuff that infuriates the "liberation" woman and delights the male chauvinist! But for you and me, it brings honest questions. What's going on here?

Well, first, there's nothing in these verses to apologize for except: (1) the *misunderstanding* that has shrouded them; and (2) the *abusive applications* they've experienced. But what *God* says and how *people* apply it are often two very different things.

At first glance, "relationship with one's wife" hardly seems to be the topic of the text, for on the face it appears to say, "Ladies shut up, the man's in charge." But, of course, that's not what's being said at all.

Though "friendship" is not specifically spelled out here, a key in *relationship* is. Take a close look with me, because there's a principle found here on how a unique partnership may take place. *Let me say that again. You can find a key here to special relationship--a holy partnership--between a man and his wife!*

To begin, let's do some spade work with this text, studying two pivotal words. The first is, *"silence,"* occurring twice in verses 11 and 12; the other is *"man,"* at the end of verse 12; and when these are clarified in this text (just like the "braids" question), things become clear and practical.

a. Defining "Silence"

"Silence" (vv. 11, 12) is the Greek word *hesuchia*, which also is used in verse 2 of this chapter. Here prayer is encouraged that we may lead a "quiet" life. Obviously, the idea of "quiet" is not "speechlessness," but controlled speech.

Clearly, the intent of the appeal to women (wives) is not a demand for a corked-mouth or strapped-shut jaws. This is not a prohibition of speech, but rather this has to do with a quietness of demeanor; a call to not being "mouthy"--neither pushy, brash or haranguing.

b. Defining "Man"

Concerning the word "man," there are two Greek words; the most familiar being "anthropos" (from which we derive anthropology, the study of mankind). "Anthropos" occurs over 500 times in the New Testament. It's the most common word for "man," referring to man as (1) the male of the species, or (2) to mankind as a race. It's used both ways.

But far more specific in designating "man" is the word *aner*, which occurs here. *Aner* appears about 250 times in the Greek New Testament; and about 50 of those times it's translated "husband." Thus, when it's put together, this passage is clearly describing a husband-wife relationship (see vs. 15, "if they"). So it is, that verse 11 should read as a *marital* reference to couples, not as a *gender* reference to the total society. Please see this: the text is discussing something between husbands and wives in their relationship; God isn't telling every woman in the world she can't say anything if there's a man around.

So, we read, "Let a *wife* learn in silence with all submission and I do not permit a *wife* to teach or have authority over her husband but to control her speech."

This spade work isn't a construction of

my own. We're simply looking at what was obviously intended by the original text. However, someone may ask, "If that's true, why hasn't it been translated that way?"

In answering, I'm embarrassed to admit why I think it hasn't been, but I'll venture the following. I think it's because the Church is *still* going through a process of reformation--of recovering things lost during the Dark Ages. There's been an ongoing restoration taking place in the Church--ever since the 16th century. What was lost, polluted, corrupted or confused spanning well over a thousand years of Church history, is *still* undergoing rediscovery and recovery. So, with reference to this particular text, and the fact that some sectors in the Church persist with a low-grade chauvinism, the translation survives its near medieval form.

And please know this: In making this re-translation, correctly substituting "wife" for "woman," I'm not espousing or surrendering to some contemporary cause. I feel little obligation to sympathize with the feminist agenda. However, these words have a practical reason; one that's not oppressing but which can be releasing for the husband and the wife *both!* So, now let's decide *why* verses 11 and 12 are here, and *how* they can work out in practical experience.

3. *Why the "Silence" Can Be Golden*

The whole intent of these verses unfolds with simplicity and clarity when the issues we've just discussed are resolved. Paul is dealing with a very human set of facts about our distinctiveness as men and women.

Women, by nature, tend to be far more intuitive, sensitive, and responsive to spiritual things than men. In comparison, if there's a countering distinctive with men, it's almost solely in the advantage of their physical make-up--primarily muscular strength. In other words, men are usually stronger physically than women, and women are usually more spiritually responsive than men.

Now, I am not saying that women have more spiritual potential than men, but that they are generally far more responsive. Women have a far greater readiness to "hear" the things of God, to accept them and put them to application. It seems then that Paul, knowing this, is seeking to assist toward a climate in which a husband will more readily accept his spiritual responsibility. In that quest, he basically is saying, "Ladies, for there to come the maximizing of what God wants to do in the church, in your home, in your community, in your husband, you're going to have pull in the reins on your spiritual oratory. Because if you, however sincerely, get pushy with him or drill him about 'spiritual stuff,' he's going to with-

48

draw even further."

Paul, still continuing with the wives, seems to be adding: "Dear lady, your husband probably already feels like something of a spiritual wimp, so don't compound it! He's never going to rise to the dynamic things of the spiritual realm and the Kingdom of God if he feels that somehow he's forever trapped far behind you. Your 'talking too much' may work against your and his best interest; only making him feel all the more a spiritual failure, and stifling his will to seek to grow."

I think the whole context of the New Testament shows that that's why Paul is saying this: "I don't want a woman to boss or cajole her husband, because I want him to learn to accept his leadership role. If she accepts it because he resigns it, he's never going to catch up." Sadly, since women are fully and equally *capable* of leadership, too many men are willing to forfeit their responsibility. By nature, they will tend to say, "Go ahead, honey--do all you want spiritually, but just keep it easy for me." But a woman controls the "gold"--the "silence" of a self-controlled bearing that can help her husband grow unto acceptance of spiritual responsibility!

Most men don't actually say, "Make it easy for me, I want to forfeit my role to my wife." And I'm not accusing any man of slothfulness, but it *is* clear that when it comes to responsible spiritual leadership, we men tend to avoid our leadership call. So the text encourages women to hold their natural tendencies in reserve, never to discourage her gifts being realized and surfacing; but rather, to point to the long-range benefit to them both if the wife will accept God's terms requiring this self-discipline.

So there *is* a call to "friendship" between husband and wife in this text. And once the relationship of husband and wife comes into alignment with God's order, amazing things happen. Where it's needed, a new joy and fruitfulness begin to be found in the marriage--something some never dreamed possible. And where they've been present, hell's flames will be extinguished in that home due to a new spiritual partnership. A new establishing of God's will--a virtual "heaven on earth"--can happen in the home, because the two are now learning a walk in spiritual and marital unity. It's a prerequisite to His Kingdom coming and dwelling in power in a home, a marriage, and a family.

So, our "difficult" passage (hopefully better understood now) points to something wonderful. And winding it up, verse 15 shows God's power and blessing working in the midst of such marital unity!

"Nevertheless she will be saved in childbearing if they continue in faith, love, holiness with self-control."

This verse refers to the Old Testament

story of sin's original impact on our race. The magnitude of that event transcends comprehension, for we have no idea what life must have been like before the Fall! But Genesis 3:16 shows that the bearing of children before the Fall might have been an easier thing for the woman. Today, of course, the majority of births come forth with great pain and travail, and the text is offering the prospect of some degree of "release" from this aspect of childbirth. So, at least at this point, a possible blessing awaits the couple who are learning the dimensions of spiritual unity we have been discussing. We are *not* told that *all* removal of birth's pain in travail is promised. So, if your wife has a difficult delivery, your or her godliness is not in question, nor is your marriage relationship necessarily being reflected upon by that fact.

But what *is* said is that there are scriptural conditions which can be met, "that they continue in faith, love and holiness with self-control." And the promise seems to indicate that when such growing mutuality occurs, *something beyond the curse* becomes released to them in their union.

Let's read it again, inserting what we've learned:

"*She,* (the wife) *will be saved* (released from the Fall's impact on childbearing) *if they* (the husband and wife) *continue together* (in growing partnership) *in faith, love, and holiness, with self-control* (basic disciplines of Christian growth)."

Looking at this promise, "something wonderful" seems to be being hinted at. If the power of Christ's redeeming work can impact the birthing process of a couple who are learning God's order together, might there be a more general blessing of "release" awaiting them? In Ephesians 5:20-33, where the flow of the husband's Christ-like "ministry" to his wife is shown for all its dynamic potential, another New Testament text points to brighter horizons. Between these two passages, I think God's Word reveals a progressing benediction of God's grace bringing couples beyond the impact of the curse in allowing for a "new beginning" of the husband-wife relationship. May I suggest that if a woman's bearing of children may be blessed, assisted, and advanced with greater ease because of the partnership she and her husband grow into, could the whole of the husband's/wife's "life-productivity" be affected? In other words, might all aspects of their life and destiny be "released" to broader dimensions of love, unity, and fulfillment *all because the husband (with her sensitive assistance) rises to fill his place in God's order?*

Here are some thoughts then, rooted in the *whole* of the Word, which convert a *problematic*, apparently legalistic text, to a *promise-filled*, life-giving one! Here are blessings of life-wide proportions; rich potentials when a husband and wife come into a growing "friendship." However, it's all contingent on the man taking his place.

My Personal Illustration:
Getting Checked About the Checks

Let me give a very simple example of "how" we men tend to resign responsibilities for "leading," and how this stresses marriages. The case may seem mundane, but maybe it can help you, Sir, to envision ways *you* need to accept responsibilities you might have neglected.

Years ago, during the first dozen years of our marriage, I would regularly bring my paycheck home and simply give it to Anna. *She* would deposit it, and *she* would pay the bills.

To my mind, this was right. It was her duty: "That's part of her job in keeping the house." And further, I felt that in giving her the money, I was displaying obvious trust in her. (How grand I thought I was! But I was later to discover it was not all that grandiose.)

Now, my wife is an intelligent woman. She was an honors graduate from college and is also experienced in bookkeeping, having done such work in a doctor's office before she and I were married. So when the problems arose in our "money matters"--and my, did they!-- it certainly wasn't due to an incapability on her part in managing the checkbook. But things degenerated. We both alternated feeling angry about it. The "money" task became an unexplainably difficult thing for her. She became very emotional, to a point that neither of us could explain it. There was no failure on her part--it wasn't that the checkbook didn't balance or that we got into trouble. But it did *weigh* on her, very heavily, and I was increasingly unsettled in my feelings about our finances (though it wasn't debt or neglect--just sensing "something's not right.")

Then one day, the Lord began dealing with me about what I was doing; or rather what I *wasn't* doing. He revealed to my understanding the REAL reason I was having her do the checkbook and taking care of paying the bills. It had been subconscious, but beneath it all I wasn't being trusting, generous or "grand." In actuality, the real reason I had assigned her the job was: *I didn't want the work or the responsibility!*

That's all there was to it.

Because I hadn't completely recognized it, I had never said, "Honey, you do this because I don't want to." I didn't even perceive my neglect--my forfeit of duty. But the Lord had begun to show me *very emphatically* that I was resigning a place of responsible leadership; that this was *something we were supposed to be doing together* instead of my casting the burden on her shoulders--a burden never intended for her to bear alone. (I must pause here, to touch on the opposite extreme. I ran into a guy one time who had the idea that taking the leadership in his household finances was to "control it all." He was the stingiest dude you ever ran across; doling money to his wife like each dime was an ingot of gold from Fort Knox. So here and now, let me emphasize, I am NOT talking about anything like that in my illustration. I'm talking about a partnership and understanding between couples, with a man learning to take his responsibilities.)

In Anna's and my case, when I took a place of responsible leadership and partnership, *everything* changed. It's something she remembers well. To say "new friendship happened" isn't off the mark. Struggling--in this case, over money matters--ceased dramatically. She grew happier all the time. And we had no explanation for this other than "something was released" when I owned up to a responsibility I had unwittingly forfeited.

The principle I'm illustrating is this: *When a man partners with his wife, a deeper union--yes, "new friendship"--can develop.* So ask the Holy Spirit to teach you practical ways to accept your leadership responsibilities. He will. And from that point, you can find new ways to grow with your wife "in faith, love, holiness and self-control" and *blessing will burst forth!* The effects of man's Fall through sin begin to be set into reverse.

That's called *"redemption!"* It's what this world, burned out from Adam I, is crying out for. People want to see it, and when they see that it's possible in you, Sir, they'll want to experience it themselves.

So, Paul's 1 Timothy 2 picture of a "holy-hands-man" is anything but the picture of the religious prude or a pious bigot. A stance of openness--of friendship and intimacy with God, turns a man into a person whose warmth of relationship with God overflows into a warmth of relationship with those in closest proximity with him--especially his wife. His growth into a husband's God-given role of leadership in the home brings comfort and peaceableness to the woman he loves.

TALK ABOUT IT! Chapter questions to discuss with a friend.

1) Because of the unique nature of this more demanding study portion of our book, consider rereading this chapter noting the following:

a) What the Bible *really* says about a woman's appearance and dress; i.e., that He doesn't prohibit loveliness--only carnal appearance.

b) What the Bible *really* says about a woman being "silent."

c) What the Bible *really* means in urging a woman's reserve in speech, so as not to discourage her husband's spiritual responsiveness.

2) Take time to discuss your own thoughts as to how the "release" potential of a husband and wife "continuing together" according to 1 Timothy 2:15 could affect your relationship.

CHAPTER FIVE:

IRON SHARPENING IRON

Please believe this: The Bible shows that *a man who would become the maximum person God can cause him to become is a man who discovers the power and blessing of partnership with other men!*

That's the principle moving us as we look at the third type of relationship key to our "becoming." To our relationships with God and our spouse, we add our relationships with men.

Now there's nothing explicit in our 1 Timothy, chapter 2 passage about relationship or friendship with other men. But what *is* in this text, is what I believe explains the reason why men usually avoid relating to other men; why men tend to "go it alone." If we can see *what* that may be--see *what* obstructs our willingness to open up to moving into partnership with other men--then maybe we can get over one of our greatest hurdles and begin to develop as fully growing men.

Jesus established this need for partnering,

man-to-man relationships on New Testament terms. He, Himself, gathered a dozen men together--shaping them to become shapers of the whole world, and their impact has continued right to this present day. Thus, "gathering men, for the sake of shaping them through interaction with one another under God, was initiated by Jesus. And that's your and my call!! Whether we are pastors of a church, new believers in Christ, men of long-term knowing God, guys wanting to influence our friends for the better--the *breakthrough* happens when we *break out* of isolation!

Contrary to popular belief, men aren't born. *Children* are born--men are *formed*. And the Bible says men help "form" each other: "As iron sharpens iron, so a man sharpens his friend" (Proverbs 27:17).

Carved, designed, and shaped--males are processed into true manhood. At the core of that process is one crucial component: man-to-man relationship. Prioritizing the cultivation of such relationships according to God's created order is in line with His blueprint for full manhood.

Ah, but we've hit a snag right there; snagged on the word "manhood." For many of us, the very term "manhood" may cause us to squirm, because it carries emotional baggage for some, and possibly conveys unachievable responsibility to others. Say the word "manhood" and some men may immediately recall the times in his childhood when he was picked last for the baseball team. Or it may bring back the fresh emotions of last month when he was laid off at work--"How can I face my peers as a failure?!" Say "manhood" and some women may instantly feel complex emotional recollections of all the times their "manly" husbands forced their desires and preferences on them to the annihilation of their own sensitivities or feelings.

"Manhood," for many simply lacks a definition with substance and value. Everybody knows what Indiana Jones is made of: guts and glory--we've seen it big and loud on the screen. But for something as basic as street-level, life-in-the-real-world "manhood," the kind that successfully functions on a daily basis within every venue of life, definitions are obscure. So in seeking to be God's man in a confused, sometimes oppressive world, some men simply choose to "give it my best, and wish for better." And there *is* a way to the "better." A living way.

The Process Of Becoming

True manhood is resourced in Jesus Christ. Don't let the simplicity of that statement blow by you. Since it *sounds* "religious" it might only conjure a mental dullness toward its earth-moving potential. But religious rhetoric doesn't change lives, God's *reality*--living truth does, and Jesus Himself is Truth Incarnate. *His indwelling your manhood is what this book is about.* He is the only salvation for a battered or ambiguous male identity, and He's the provider of substance to bring definition to your manhood and mine.

It's God's intent to reproduce Jesus in us: "For it was fitting for Him, for whom are all things and by whom are all things, in bringing many sons to glory, to make the captain of their salvation perfect through sufferings" (Heb. 2:10).

That's God's design--getting the glorious image of Jesus Christ to be reproduced in any person who will ask Him to do so. It works for *both* genders! In Christ, women can be *truly* liberated and celebrated, and in Him men can finally escape the world of "self-help" programs and *machismo* power tactics. However, being conformed into the image of Jesus can't be done Lone Ranger style. One of the chief scalpels that God has chosen for shaping us into His image is the dynamic of personal friendships--man-to-man relationships. This is an essential, practical biblical principle, and one of a man's key starting places.

More Than A Greeting Card

Friendships not only reflect the man, but they can make him what he is. They form him. They decide his depth, his qualities, his skills and his destiny, for we're told, "He who walks with wise men will be wise, but

61

the companion of fools will be destroyed" (Prov. 13:20).

The topic of "friendship" could smack of something perceived only at the Hallmark card level--a nice word with nice sentiments. But the irresistible force and life-destiny-impact of "friendships" is more than a greeting card concept. We dare not overlook it, especially as men committed to Christ's man-to-man methods. How many of us--do you?--tend to find escape routes seeking to insulate us from encounters or relation-ships calling us to man-to-man commit-ment. That course forward toward relation-ships may make us feel our real identities are threatened, tempting us, instead, to buy into those things which only feed our fanta-sies. But what we need for starters is to move toward personal honesty with ourselves and others into friendships/relationships which foster transparency and identity-renovating selflessness.

Can faking the appearance of "having it all together" be more important to me than the actuality of my being available to being "sharpened" into Christ's image? I hope not! Because for me to be available for growth means for me to be willing to admit need.

That's not very macho, is it?

Yet admission of our needs seems to be at the core of God's dealing with humanity--from coming to an altar and admitting my need for the Savior, to learning to "confess your faults to one another, and pray for one another, that you may be healed" (James 5:16). So, for starts, I simply need to admit my need for partnership with other people--other men--in order to advance with Christ and grow in Jesus victoriously.

There's a profound shaping of men that happens when we *come together* and learn to *grow together* in Christ. John wrote these words, "If we walk in the light as He (Christ) is in the light, then we will have fellowship one with another."

Notice: if we'll get together (true "fellowship" in Christ) there's something that will happen to us all--"The blood of Jesus Christ *keeps on cleansing us from all sin!*" That's the way the tense in the original Greek text puts it!

Progressing in fellowship brings progression in victory over sin's clutchings at a man's body, soul, and spirit!! In other words, as we--you and I--walk in the light with other brothers, there is a *progressive sense* of what has already been *positionally secured* in Christ. Your and my *past* sin was totally covered, atoned for in Christ, and forgiven completely when we came to Him. But *present* sin still finds occasions to tempt and try us. Our humanness is not overthrown because we received Christ. That doesn't diminish the reality of our salvation, but present sin must be faced and dealt with. That's why, in walking with Jesus, I need to also walk with my brothers in Him--to "walk in the light" of a growing relationship of friendship, partnership, and accountability.

As a result, through a loving and brotherly confronting of one another--not with ridicule but with honest-to-God, face-to-face realism--our trusting transparency ("in the light") *advances* the work of righteousness in each of us. Through our "fellowship with one another" we can discover a special operation of the sanctifying blood of Christ. The promise here declares it, and it's progressive in its ongoing work: "The blood of Jesus, His Son, *keeps on cleansing me* from all sin!" (Paraphrase, 1 John 1:8). We'll study this pathway to such transparency and accountability in another of our *Power To Become* books for men, but first we each need to decide to *accept the terms* of such a need for "friendship with other men."

We need one another.

That's the reason for men's gatherings--large and small--among Christ's own! Nothing is a greater passion with me. In my own pastorate, I would even sacrifice Sunday morning preaching if I needed to, in order to meet with the men of my church. Thankfully I don't have to make that choice, but my priorities are clear. I want to touch the point from which everything springs: *Men.*

As pivotally important and essentially necessary as this "man-to-man relationship" need is, and as clear-in-the-Bible it is shown to be Jesus' method, hosts of men never allow themselves to become subject to that kind of possibility for fellowship. So often, a men's fellowship in the Church of Jesus Christ becomes only a kind of "hail fellow well-met" get-together--paint a building, mow a lawn, play on a team, even have a Bible study.

Those, of course, are all good things for men to do. But men's activities are not a substitute for men coming together and interfacing at a personal, spiritual dimension. There's a reason why this doesn't happen more commonly. And as we move toward conclusion of this study, let me tell you why I think we men back away from openness toward each other.

TALK ABOUT IT! Chapter questions to discuss with a friend.

1) Describe the relationship between the power of "the blood of Jesus" and "walking in the light" with your brothers. What is "walking in the light"?

2) Have you identified your own reactions, if any, to the mention of the word "manhood"?

3) In what ways, no matter how small, have you felt tempted to "go it alone" when you really should have relied on brothers in Christ? Identify "excuses" which preempt your involvements.

CHAPTER SIX:

BECOMING INSTRUMENTS OF HIS REDEMPTIVE POWER

We're finding our starting place in partnership with God's. Since He's determined to make men His catalysts in the broad extension in His Kingdom purposes--from personal levels, to family, to the church, to the world--how can we cooperate? The answer to that question is in discovering keys to relationships. And now, we've come to the place of seeing how you and I can overcome our greatest hindrance to becoming "relational" men.

We have asked, "Why don't we men more readily open to relationships?" I think our text contains an insightful fact about us men; one which points to the heart of our problem in "getting together" and thereby in our "getting *IT* together." Look at our text:

"But Adam was not deceived but the woman being deceived fell into transgression" (1 Timothy 2:14).

There is something far more poignant about these words than meets the eye of the casual reader. Ask yourself, why is this reference to the original sin made here? And, why is the role of each--a man and woman--noted separately from one another in their transgression? In answering this, look first at how Adam and his wife are each described as participating in the Fall of the human race into sin.

• *The man*--Was not deceived, he consciously disobeyed (verse 14; also see Rom. 5:19);

• *The woman*--Being deceived, she fell into sin (verse 14; also see Gen. 3:1-6).

These are radically different descriptions, which I am persuaded the Holy Spirit has given for important reasons. This distinction unlocks a perspective to which I invite you; one which can help us not only see what the original man might have become, but what we as redeemed men *can* become.

If I recall *any* observations on this tender passage in verse 14, it's usually been tied to the earlier "prohibition" regarding women speaking. The intimation has always seemed to be that, somehow, "The woman was deceived" because women are gullible, if not stupid. "Look how the serpent deceived her," I've heard preachers intone. To hear them one would think there has never been such a thing as a *man* being deceived! But every one of us knows the opposite is true--we've all been deceived! And there is no way that "the woman being deceived" can be construed to suggest women, generically, are any less intelligent or sensible than men, then or now. So what *is* the point? The point is that the Bible is pressing a significant issue into view.

Look at the awesome issue which distills from distinguishing the role of each of the first couple in the Fall. In this passage:

(a) *which is describing God's desire to see men stand forth in bold relationship with Him;* and

(b) *which is urging women to relate to their husbands in a way that will increase the likelihood of their responsiveness toward God.*

Here, the Holy Spirit notes an important difference between men and women. It's this: When the Fall of the first couple occurred, the most guilty party was the man, who consciously disobeyed. This is not to imply the woman was less sinful, but the text clearly states she was motivated differently on that occasion than the man. She was a victim of deception, not *conscious* disobedience: in stark, biblical contrast "Adam was not deceived," but *consciously rebelled.*

Again, let me stress that this distinction is not to imply that either Adam or his wife were more or less guilty than the other in the final analysis. But I believe in this text the Holy

Spirit has provided an important insight which seems intended to open our understanding. It is here we are given understanding as to why men are so slow to open themselves to God, to their wives, to each other; and why women seem not to share this reluctance.

I think God's Word discloses right here an answer to our peculiarities within our genders. I don't think it's a factor consciously responded to, but a study of our humanity--male and female--certainly confirms the likelihood that a *spiritual imprint* is carried in our souls which differs at the point of our God-responsiveness. Women, almost uniformly, respond more readily to spiritual matters, to God's Word, and to one another in general than men tend to do. Men, almost uniformly, withdraw or retire from spiritual matters, openness to God, and from one another.

I want to suggest that deep within the psyche of every man, though undiscerned and unlearned, there is a residue of subconscious remembrance that he--the man--is *more responsible* for the Fall of the race than the woman. It appears that men bear a *spiritual imprint* which is almost haunting in nature, as though to say, "Sir, in the person of your 'megagreat' grandfather Adam, you failed *in the light* of 'knowing better.' It's too late! You fouled your chance, so *never* embarrass yourself again by opening to that 'light'; you'll only fail again!"

70

"But wait," someone cries, "the woman partook of the fruit first!" And that, of course, is true. But come with me back to the Garden scene. It's there that I want to take a fresh look at the event of the Fall of man; to see what *did* happen and what *might* have happened.

What Did Happen?

According to Genesis chapter 3, the woman, when confronted by a satanic incarnation in the form of a serpent was completely deceived by the devil. As we have noted, this is no argument against her being fully responsible for her sin. But we have also noted, the *climate* of her consciousness was one of passive delusion rather than one of aggressive disobedience, and she ate the fruit. Imagine the setting:

"My," she sighs. "I...I..." she speaks, bewildered by the change coming over her; attempting to interpret the moment, exclaims, "It certainly *tastes* good!" Her thoughts begin to frame the patterns of fallenness: "My goodness, what sudden insight. I don't know why we ever hesitated!" Here's the victim of deception, musing over the moment. Deceived, and now sin-bound.

The brevity of the biblical text does not provide a timing sequence for us, but it was apparently soon thereafter when she brought the fruit to her husband. And Adam ate it.

71

It is at this point we join the revelation of the Genesis record to the words of our text in 1 Timothy. According to the Scripture we are told that Adam sinned, *not* as deceived, but as consciously disobedient. The man *knew full well what he was doing.* Probably not present at all at the time of the woman's temptation, and thereby not beguiled by the serpent, here he is--looking face to face with the woman's offer: "To sin or not to sin."

Eve's approach isn't to be blamed. It isn't as though she said, "Come on, *sin!*" But, far more likely, she came to Adam with something more on the order of an approach born of her bewilderment and newly-fallen state of mind: "My husband, this is not the evil we thought it was. Come and take some of this for wisdom's sake."

But Adam knew better, and in his sinning he disobeyed as one undeceived--with his eyes wide open.

A Different Garden Scenario

But what *might* have happened in the Garden? What if Adam had responded another way--a redemptive way--when Eve had fallen? When he saw her coming, when he heard her speak, what might he have said instead? Instead, imagine him--broken and with tears--crying, "Oh, my beloved! Why, oh why? You ate it! Death has already begun in you, and you are blind to it. Oh, my dear one, you are going to die! No, my wife! As

72

dearly as I love you, I cannot--I will not violate the Creator's will. I *will* not eat of this fruit!"

And there, suddenly, she would have stood nakedly aware of what she had done. Now the charm of the serpent's device has been blown away, and she leaves the scene, overcome with a deep sense of shame. Then...

Coming now in the cool of the day, the Father of all Creation approaches Adam. And as Adam prepares to meet Him at their usual time of fellowship, the Father sees a pained expression on Adam's face. He asks, "Adam, where is the woman?" And even before Adam responds, the Father says, "She has eaten the forbidden fruit, hasn't she?"

"Yes, Father."

Silence. Then...Heaven's Lover speaks: "Then she must die." And there is nothing but broken-hearted love in the Father's voice as he says it.

"But Father," the man implores, "I love her." A pause, and again, "I love her...and *I don't want her to die!*" Tears fill human eyes for the first time, as the man weeps with an impending sense of loss.

The Father replies: "I understand. And I would wish her to live as well. But the eternal decree requires it. She must die." There is another moment of pained silence, then the Creator speaks again: "Yes, I weep too, but she must die: that is, O Adam, *unless another dies for her--in her place.*"

And the man, at first surprised--but then with understanding of the divine economy, looks up. With a firm resolve and a readiness of response; not with haste but with a measured cadence, now having dried his eyes, he speaks: "Then, Father, let *me* be the one. I will take her place in death, for I love her and long that she not be stolen unto death by the evil one."

"But wait!" someone shouts. "How can you create this story! On what authority do you propose such a possibility might have been present?" And my answer is:

Because that's the way The Story actually goes. Not, of course, that the *First* Adam fulfilled his leadership role as the one who "was created first"; *not* that through obedience and sacrifice he became an instrument of redemption.

No. The *First* Adam forfeited that role through *disobedience.* But the *Second* Adam came, and He *did* die! And He died on behalf of one whom He calls *His* Bride, His Church, *so that she may live and not die.* Jesus Christ fulfilled the redemptive role which today is made the model for the redeemed man's relationship with his wife: "...Husbands, love your wives as Christ loved the Church and gave Himself for her" (Eph. 5:25). But not only do men rarely fulfill this role, we also shrink from man-to-man commitments which would help us grow in our potential as leaders who minister redemption's grace and power to others. It seems that somehow all sons of the first Adam sense that our earthly forefather has bequeathed a failure to us. It seems that as men we somehow have had a scar burned into our collective masculine psyche; a sense of disability fulfilling our spiritual role; a subtle inner voice which shouts, "Your father failed as a man and so will you! He missed becoming an instrument of redemption, and neither will you ever be able to become an instrument in God's hands!"

Even when we each receive the salvation brought to us by Adam II--the Lord Jesus Christ, Son of God (1 Cor. 15:22), the lingering, inherent sense of our violated role as "man" haunts us. Farcical renditions of the original sin story--shallow joking of, "Well, the woman ate first"--still disallow our escape from the fact that even though she was deceived, it was the *man* who consciously disobeyed; who forfeited obedience, embraced his own way, and learned nothing of a role he might have in redemptive possibilities. (And in passing, may we witness the incredible grace of God toward womankind, hearing the Lord say of the deceived woman "Of *her* seed the serpent's head will be crushed"--Gen. 3:15; granting her a role in redemption's processes.)

Yes, *both* sinned.

Yes, *both* will need salvation. And *both* will taste of grace as surely as they tasted of sin's fruit.

But the stamp has cut deep in the souls of the male of the species. The die of death has been cut, and remade us over and over again: men who fail their role. You see, my brothers, everything around us tends to argue toward our repeated fallibility. It timelessly tends to discourage our readiness to respond: "I don't want to open up to other brothers, because then it calls me all over again--(1) to *obedience* and (2) to *become an instrument of redemption.*"

But instead--now, please--listen to me; and *come!*

Let us each be shaken free of the cowardice that lurks in every one of our souls because of the failure of our distant father, Adam. *Through Jesus our Savior, we have been born of a new Father; and He is able to restore, renew, rebuild, and release us!*

There is *another* Adam; Christ our Living Lord. His name is Jesus, and He's come to *live in you and me.* By His power He can enable my obedience and my openness to become an instrument of His redemptive grace. With resurrection mightiness He will work in and through us, *reproducing* the fullness of His life; not only in *cleansing* of our soul with saving blood to assure us of heaven, but in *overflowing* our being with His personal presence--*dwelling* within us to nurture our growth and to impact our world through us!

I call you, dear brother, my friend, to learn the way of relationship; of friendship with the Father, of friendship with your wife, and of friendship with other brothers, so that you can become the maximum man God wants you to be. And as that begins, you will find a new release start in things around you. Results are not always immediate, but the impact will begin to become manifest: in your home, your relationships, your business, your church...and your world. God grant that it be so. Pray with me:

"Lord, I yearn to be free from the failure-scarred image of Adam. Not that sinless perfection can be mine this side of heaven, but in order that sin's crippling impact upon my male psyche would be reversed and so that I can be transformed into the likeness of Christ, I now invite You to move in my heart. I give Your Holy Spirit permission to work in me as it pleases You. I ask that You would *create within me* a new understanding of my role as a man according to Your original design in creation. And I ask that You would *release through me* Your leadership dynamic to be expressed in love, power, sensitivity, and wisdom to everyone I contact. In short, Father, please come and dwell in the midst of every relationship I have. Let me become an effective instrument of Your redemption; certainly in my family, but also among my friends, with other men, within the business community, and everywhere I go. Lord, Your Kingdom come, Your will be done on earth--here where I live and move every day--just as it is in heaven. Amen."

TALK ABOUT IT! Chapter questions to discuss with a friend.

1) On what grounds is the possibility proposed that Adam might have become a "savior" of his fallen spouse?

2) In what ways can a man still "die" for his wife--selflessly laying down his life for hers?

3) Describe where you would like the Lord to free you from bondage patterns of your family.

IT'S ALL IN THE "DOING"

Receiving biblical teaching with an open heart is vital. But *"doing it"*--putting legs on the truth you've learned--is Christianity.

A national ad campaign for a line of sports shoes recently used a direct command for its sales pitch: "Just Do It!" It aptly reflected the spirit of the competitive edge. For no race is won by mere philosophy or good thoughts--you have to DO it--which in our spiritual race means: get off the proverbial couch, move from the prescribed Starting Place and press toward the mark of our high calling down the King's Highway!

Application: get with men. On a regular basis, meet with several men with whom you can (a) generate mutual, consistent support in prayer, (b) teach one another things the Lord is showing you in your life, and (c) learn a new level of transparency in the process.

We strongly encourage each of you reading these words to prayerfully select several brothers with whom you can meet at breakfast on a regular basis. We say "breakfast" as a suggestion because an early meeting can often clear most busy schedules; and we say "regular" because that's how trust can be developed within your group.

Jesus exampled for us *breakfast time* transformed into *discipling time*. John chapter 21 is a precious passage about the Risen Lord and his relationship with His disciples. The trauma of the cross behind Him, and the glory of the resurrection accomplished, Jesus didn't meet His disciples that morning amid some awe-inspiring Transfiguration-like glory, or on a mountain top with lightning and thunder rumbling about. Instead, He fixed breakfast for them...a very "family" thing to do. He "dined" with them and it was intimate and relational. Springing out from this fellowship setting, Jesus discussed with Peter a top priority on His mind: *the importance of feeding the sheep*.

Breakfast. Feeding the sheep. There's a message there.

The *occasion* is discipling fellowship at breakfast, the *agenda* is nourishing the sheep at our table--us included.

And it can change your life. Because Jesus is there.

In setting up such a meeting time with some brothers, here's a few considerations to keep in mind:

1) Find some brothers with whom you feel

free to be open and candid about your own areas of need and struggle. But don't let the group get too large. The bigger it is the tougher it is to really "open up." Target size: 3-4 men.

2) Set a regular meeting time once or twice a week.

3) Agree together that you are committing to meet weekly for a season of time, say, for four months.

4) Pray for each other. Share your struggles and victories together.

5) You may want to consider using the devotional on the following pages as a spring board for discussion. And, in essence, fulfill the Lord's command to "feed my sheep." God has ordained that we men be leaders. But we're also His sheep.

So, "let's do lunch" . . . (or breakfast). . . and then link arms, join hearts, and put our shoe leather into the race of "becoming" men who look unto Jesus, the Author and Finisher of our faith as we grow together!

DEVOTIONS
IN THE BOOK OF 1 SAMUEL

Contributed by Bob Anderson

The following devotional is designed for stimulating discussion and prayer within a small group of men.

1 Samuel was chosen because it provides a rich reference for studying relationships. In fact, it reads somewhat like a good screenplay: rich characters, relational conflict, struggles for power. Yet through it all, we see God's persistant faithfulness moving in the midst of imperfect humanity. And there are dynamic lessons to be learned by witnessing how God worked in the key relationships of Samuel, David, and Saul.

☐ **Today's Text: 1 Samuel 1:1-28** *(key: v. 28)*

1 **Today's Truth:** Hannah was "lending" her son, Samuel, to the Lord in dedication. But the Hebrew term for "lent" does not mean to give temporarily, but to give *unconditionally*.

Today's Thoughts:_____
_____
_____

☐ **Today's Text: 1 Samuel 2:1-36** *(key v.18)*

2 **Today's Truth:** Samuel's childlike openness to the Lord was a condition of heart he never outgrew.

Today's Thoughts:_____
_____
_____

☐ **Today's Text: 1 Samuel 3:1-21** *(key v. 20)*

3 **Today's Truth:** Samuel's pattern of waiting tenderheartedly upon the Lord in private, eager to hear His voice, eventually resulted in a national promotion from the Hand of Omnipotence.

Today's Thoughts:_____
_____
_____

☐ **Today's Text: 1 Samuel 4:1-22** *(key v. 22)*

4 **Today's Truth:** Christ in us is our hope of glory. Though the devil can't separate us from the love of God in Christ, he *does* try to diminish God's glory in us by stealing our confidence in our foundational identity in Christ.

Today's Thoughts: _____

_____

_____

☐ **Today's Text: 1 Samuel 5:1-12** *(key v. 4)*

5 **Today's Truth:** The "mere" presence of God in a place topples the powers of hell. And the presence of God is most forcefully fostered when God's people worship Him.

Today's Thoughts: _____

_____

_____

☐ **Today's Text: 1 Samuel 6:1-21** *(key v. 19a)*

6 **Today's Truth:** These men looked for or sought out the power of the ark instead of God's presence. God's call to us is always for relationship, not for seeking spiritual power.

Today's Thoughts: _____

_____

_____

☐ **Today's Text: 1 Samuel 7:1-17** *(key v. 12)*

7 **Today's Truth:** Samuel set up a stone of testimony saying, "Thus far the Lord has helped us." Following his example is wise: keeping a personal record of God's faithfulness to be remembered at future times of discouragement can bring renewal of strength.

Today's Thoughts: _____

_____

_____

☐ **Today's Text: 1 Samuel 8:1-22** *(key vv. 19-20)*

8 **Today's Truth:** Israel cried out, "We want to be just like other nations!" and it became a horrendous snare to them. Embracing conformity to this corrupt world brings defeat.

Today's Thoughts: _____

_____

_____

☐ **Today's Text: 1 Samuel 9:1-27** *(key v. 20b)*

9 **Today's Truth:** Israel's desire was for Saul, a leader who "looked good" (see 1 Sam. 10:23-24). We would later see God's idea of a king: David, a man after His own heart.

Today's Thoughts: _____

_____

_____

☐ **Today's Text: 1 Samuel 10:1-27** *(key v. 6)*

10 **Today's Truth:** Saul was filled with the Spirit of God and changed into a new man. The sobering reality is: he didn't *stay* changed by walking closely with his Lord.

Today's Thoughts: _____

_____

_____

☐ **Today's Text: 1 Samuel 11:1-15** *(key v. 14)*

11 **Today's Truth:** Samuel said it was time to "renew" the kingdom, which meant the people were to unify together to rededicate themselves to the purpose of their kingdom. Gathering with brothers at breakfast to pray is a great way to "renew God's Kingdom" in force.

Today's Thoughts: _____

_____

_____

☐ **Today's Text: 1 Samuel 12:1-25** *(key v. 20)*

12 **Today's Truth:** Samuel puts his finger on the human tendency to shy back from the Lord after we're convicted of serious sin. But God's call is for us to immediately repent, be forgiven, then resume serving Him with all our hearts.

Today's Thoughts: _____

_____

_____

☐ **Today's Text: 1 Samuel 13:1-23** *(key vv. 9-12)*

13 **Today's Truth:** Anyone in authority must also be under authority himself. Even when confronted about his wrongdoing, Saul quickly blamed everyone but himself.

Today's Thoughts: _____

_____

_____

☐ **Today's Text: 1 Samuel 14:1-52** *(key v.45)*

14 **Today's Truth:** The Lord's relationship with Jonathan took priority over Saul's rash oath even though Jonathan was technically in violation of the king's edict. God's mercy flows even when men are ready to judge and cast stones.

Today's Thoughts: _____

_____

_____

☐ **Today's Text: 1 Samuel 15:1-35** *(key v. 22)*

15 **Today's Truth:** To obey is better than sacrifice. Of course, there'll be sacrifice along the way of obeying God. But He's not looking for ways to deprive His people of good things. Ultimately, the fruit of obedience will be godliness with contentment and blessing with no sorrow added.

Today's Thoughts: _____

_____

_____

☐ **Today's Text: 1 Samuel 16:1-23** *(key v. 7)*

16 **Today's Truth:** Thank goodness--the Lord looks on the heart and not the outward appearance! It's wise to "do a heart-check" and regularly monitor our attitudes and motivations. The Psalms reveal that David did--a lot!

Today's Thoughts: _____

_____

_____

☐ **Today's Text: 1 Samuel 17:1-58** *(key v.45)*

17 **Today's Truth:** One of the greatest confrontations of all time: David & Goliath. Whether your Goliath is a financial crisis, a broken marriage, or an uncertain destiny, the battle is the Lord's. David's small stone guarantees it.

Today's Thoughts: _____

_____

_____

☐ **Today's Text: 1 Samuel 18:1-30** *(key v. 11)*

18 **Today's Truth:** Like the Kingdom of God, jealousy can start as a small mustard seed. Given place and left unchecked, it can yield murder in the heart and even become a spear in the hand. Not only confessing and forsaking sin, but praying for the further blessing of the envied person brings freedom.

Today's Thoughts: _____

_____

_____

☐
19

Today's Text: 1 Samuel 19:1-24 *(key v. 9)*

Today's Truth: God isn't hurling demons at Saul, but we see that in the absence of the Spirit of God, men are vulnerable to hell's forces--sin being the "welcome mat" for bondage.

Today's Thoughts: _____

_____

_____

☐
20

Today's Text: 1 Samuel 20:1-42 *(key v. 41)*

Today's Truth: Jonathan and David typify the amazing love God can work between men. It is a rare kind of relationship, but it's nothing beyond God's ability to work in your own experience if you simply ask Him for that caliber of friendship.

Today's Thoughts: _____

_____

_____

☐
21

Today's Text: 1 Samuel 21:1-15 *(key v. 9)*

Today's Truth: God not only gave David victory over Goliath; now the very weapon of his enemy was in his hand. We, too, are more than conquerers through Him who loves us!

Today's Thoughts: _____

_____

_____

☐ **Today's Text: 1 Samuel 22:1-23** *(key v. 22)*

22 **Today's Truth:** Amazing as it is, David claimed he was responsible for the death of the priests slain by Saul. Whereas Saul typically rolled his guilt onto others, David did the opposite. He was keenly sensitive to the impact his actions had on others. *That's* responsibility!

Today's Thoughts: _____

_____

_____

☐ **Today's Text: 1 Samuel 23:1-29** *(key v. 12)*

23 **Today's Truth:** David's acceptance of spiritual responsibility and discipline saved his life and the lives of the men with him. As priests of our home, our everyday decisions can be either life-giving or life-diminishing.

Today's Thoughts: _____

_____

_____

☐ **Today's Text: 1 Samuel 24:1-22** *(key v. 26)*

24 **Today's Truth:** David was grieved for so little as cutting Saul's robe. If we, like David, want to be a "man after God's heart," we should follow his example by not returning evil for evil.

Today's Thoughts: _____

_____

_____

☐ **Today's Text: 1 Samuel 25:1-44** *(key v. 39)*

25 **Today's Truth:** David gave room for the wrath of God. Instead of taking matters into his own hands, he let God avenge his enemies.

Today's Thoughts: _____

_____

_____

☐ **Today's Text: 1 Samuel 26:1-25** *(key v. 21)*

26 **Today's Truth:** Saul repents--the right thing to do, but far too late--after destruction has run its course and reached maturity in his life. Jesus is quick to forgive us of all sin--but why wait to repent until after seasons of sin have burned a hole in the tapestry of our lives?

Today's Thoughts: _____

_____

_____

☐ **Today's Text: 1 Samuel 27:1-12** *(key v. 9)*

27 **Today's Truth:** David's raids served as corrective surgery for future generations, slaying the evil of false demon gods along with the societies that served them. As believers we are assigned to demolish spiritual strongholds with at least as much diligence.

Today's Thoughts: _____

_____

_____

Today's Text: 1 Samuel 28:1-25 *(key v. 17)*

28

Today's Truth: Saul served as Israel's king fo 40 years. David would also reign for 40 years What made the two kings so dramatically dif ferent was their heart-responsiveness--or lack of it--towards the Lord. The final hours of each king's life reflected the decisions of a lifetime

Today's Thoughts: _____

_____

_____

Today's Text: 1 Samuel 29:1-11 *(key v. 6)*

29

Today's Truth: When a man walks closely with the Lord, even his enemies will admire his character and integrity.

Today's Thoughts: _____

_____

_____

Today's Text: 1 Samuel 30:1-31 *(key v. 6)*

30

Today's Truth: David strengthened himself in the Lord and sought His council, even when impaled by grief over a kidnapped wife and surrounded by bitter people ready to stone him to death. Accusing God or others was the furthest thing from David's lips.

Today's Thoughts: _____

_____

_____

Today's Text: 1 Samuel 31:1-13 *(key v. 6)*

31

Today's Truth: To analyze the different substances comprising Saul's heart--which led to his tragic end--and the heart of David, as imperfect as he was, may be one of the most valuable studies a man of God can make. Same occupation, same God, same nation, same historical period, same opportunities for good and evil . . . yet the two men ended up in dramatically divergent destinies. Truly, all the decisions each man made in response to the Lord throughout their lives respectively, added up to one conclusive, final bottom-line result for each.

Today's Thoughts: _____

_____

_____

_____

_____

_____

_____